First World War
and Army of Occupation
War Diary
France, Belgium and Germany

24 DIVISION
73 Infantry Brigade,
Brigade Trench Mortar Battery
5 December 1917 - 22 January 1919

WO95/2219/4

The Naval & Military Press Ltd
www.nmarchive.com
Published in association with The National Archives

Published by

The Naval & Military Press Ltd

Unit 10 Ridgewood Industrial Park,

Uckfield, East Sussex,

TN22 5QE England

Tel: +44 (0) 1825 749494

www.naval-military-press.com

www.nmarchive.com

This diary has been reprinted in facsimile from the original. Any imperfections are inevitably reproduced and the quality may fall short of modern type and cartographic standards.

© **Crown Copyright**
Images reproduced by permission of The National Archives, London, England, 2015.

Contents

Document type	Place/Title	Date From	Date To
Heading	WO95/2219/4		
Heading	73rd Lt Trench Mortar Bty Jan 1918-Jan 1919		
Heading	73rd Light Trench Mortar Battalion for the month of December 1917		
War Diary		05/12/1917	31/12/1917
Heading	73rd light Trench Mortar Battalion for the month of January 1918		
War Diary		01/01/1918	31/01/1918
Miscellaneous	Operation Orders 51	17/01/1918	17/01/1918
Operation(al) Order(s)	Operation Orders 50		
Heading	73rd Light Trench Mortar Battery for the month of February 1918		
War Diary	Hervilly	01/03/1918	14/03/1918
War Diary	Templieux	15/03/1918	28/03/1918
Heading	73rd Light Trench Mortar Battery March 1918		
Heading	73rd Light Trench Mortar Battery for the month of March 1918		
War Diary	Templeux	01/03/1918	31/03/1918
Heading	73rd Light Trench Mortar Battery for the month of April 1918		
War Diary		01/04/1918	30/04/1918
Heading	73rd Light Trench Mortar Battery for the month of May 1918		
War Diary	Hill 70 Loos	01/05/1918	28/05/1918
Heading	War Diary for month of June 73rd Light Trench Mortar Battery		
War Diary	Line	02/06/1918	06/06/1918
War Diary	Les Brebis	10/06/1918	18/06/1918
War Diary	Line	20/06/1918	30/06/1918
Heading	73rd Light Trench Mortar Battery for the month of July 1918		
War Diary	Hill 70 Loos	01/07/1918	23/07/1918
Heading	73rd Light Trench Mortar Battery for the month of August 1918		
War Diary	Hill 70	01/08/1918	27/08/1918
War Diary	Lievin	27/08/1918	31/08/1918
Heading	73rd Light T. M. Battery War Diary		
War Diary	Lens	01/09/1918	01/10/1918
Operation(al) Order(s)	73rd Light Mortar Battery Order No. 107		
Heading	73rd Light Trench Mortar Battery for the month of October 1918		
War Diary	Bout des Pres	01/10/1918	10/10/1918
War Diary	Rieux	11/10/1918	13/10/1918
War Diary	Avesnes	14/10/1918	26/10/1918
Heading	73rd Light Trench Mortar Battery for the month of November 1918		
War Diary	Haussey	01/11/1918	02/11/1918
War Diary	Bermerain	03/11/1918	03/11/1918
War Diary	Maresches	04/11/1918	04/11/1918
War Diary	Wargnies-les Petit	05/11/1918	06/11/1918

War Diary	Bavai	07/11/1918	07/11/1918
War Diary	Le Louvoin	08/11/1918	08/11/1918
War Diary	Le Basvents	09/11/1918	09/11/1918
War Diary	Floricamp		
War Diary	Fienigies	10/11/1918	10/11/1918
War Diary	Bavai Louvignies	11/11/1918	16/11/1918
War Diary	Wargnies-les Grand	17/11/1918	17/11/1918
War Diary	Provey	18/11/1918	18/11/1918
War Diary	Aniche	19/11/1918	24/11/1918
War Diary	Rumegies	25/11/1918	26/11/1918
War Diary	Mouchin	27/11/1918	30/11/1918
Heading	War Diary 73 L T M Battery		
War Diary	Mouchin	01/12/1918	18/12/1918
War Diary	Taintignes	29/12/1918	29/12/1918
Heading	73rd Light Trench Mortar Battery for the month of January 1919		
War Diary	Taintignes	02/01/1919	22/01/1919

WO 95 2219/4

24TH DIVISION
73RD INFY BDE

73RD LT TRENCH MORTAR BTY
JAN 1918 - JAN 1919

WAR DIARY
INTELLIGENCE SUMMARY.
(Erase heading not required.)

Army Form C. 2118.

Place	Date	Hour	Summary of Events and Information	Remarks and references to Appendices
Jerusalem			104th Light Trench Mortar Battery For the month of December 1917	

Army Form C. 2118.

WAR DIARY DECEMBER '17.
or
INTELLIGENCE SUMMARY.

(Erase heading not required.)

Instructions regarding War Diaries and Intelligence Summaries are contained in F. S. Regs., Part II. and the Staff Manual respectively. Title pages will be prepared in manuscript.

Place	Date	Hour	Summary of Events and Information	Remarks and references to Appendices
	5.	4pm	Intersection relief.	
	7.	1.20am	Barrage fire in conjunction with raid by 2nd LEINSTERS. 8 guns in action - Two guns on FISH LANE - one on FERRET right - two in "RUBY" & three in MALAKOFF. EXPENDITURE - 200 rounds. Casualties NIL.	
	9."	4pm	Intersection relief.	
	11."	11.30pm	Barrage fire in conjunction with raid by 9th R. SUSSEX Rt: Three guns in MALAKOFF only in action - Expenditure 75 rounds. Casualties NIL.	
	13."	4pm	Intersection relief.	
	18."	4pm	Advanced section relief. Battery was relieved by the 17th A.T.M. Batt. Ba relief the Battery moved to HERUILLY.	
	27."	—	Officers reconnoitred the positions assigned for Bn? front prior to relief.	
	30."	2.30pm	The Battery relieved the 72nd & 71st Bath. Taking over Guns in the Line.	See Appendix 1
	6.30pm opening after		20 rounds fired on working party by Nº II & III.	

Army Form C. 2118.

WAR DIARY
or
INTELLIGENCE SUMMARY.

(Erase heading not required.)

DECEMBER 1917

Place	Date	Hour	Summary of Events and Information	Remarks and references to Appendices
	29th	7pm	Gos. II - I & IV guns engaged in firing a shrapnel M.G. 7 rounds were fired & the M.G. silenced - 35 rounds fired by battery on front & support lines	
	30th		130 rounds expended on M.G. working parties etc. No IV gun unable to get onto a working party. Cpl KENNA & Pte CLARKIN dismounted the piece & took into firing position from sand bank - Cpl KENNA firing the gun whilst Pte CLARKIN held the piece between his legs - The working party was dispersed.	
	31st		103 rounds expended - Travelling M.G. was again observed. This M.G. was interfering with our wiring parties -	

Sgt Strange Lieut
o/c 73 " L.T.M.Batt

WAR DIARY
INTELLIGENCE SUMMARY.
(Erase heading not required.)

Army Form C. 2118.

Instructions regarding War Diaries and Intelligence Summaries are contained in F. S. Regs., Part II. and the Staff Manual respectively. Title pages will be prepared in manuscript.

Place	Date	Hour	Summary of Events and Information	Remarks and references to Appendices
Confidential			43rd Light Trench Mortar Battery for the month of January 1919 — Jan 1919	

WAR DIARY JANUARY 18

or

INTELLIGENCE SUMMARY

Army Form C. 2118.

Place	Date	Hour	Summary of Events and Information	Remarks and references to Appendices
	1st	5.30pm	Intersection relief. Expenditure nil.	
	2nd	8.a.	Lt. SMITH attacked Jan 13th M.K. Left this Battery to go as instructor to dismounted Cavalry - Was relieved by 2nd Lt WILLIAMS. Expenditure 58.	
	3rd		Expenditure 140 - Same M.G. was engaged again & silenced. Patrol dispersed. Slight retaliation enemy from 77m guns on Z & XI.	
	4th		Expenditure 132. Same M.G. was engaged - Patrols report Pardrell Pt were attacked & calls for help came from enfranchised - T.M. fired on retaliation on enemy starts. Lo IV dispersed a wiring party & takes a patrol.	
	5th		Expenditure 82 - Intersection.	
	6th		Intersection relief - During this tour 2/Lt WILLIAMS & Lt TOBYN were strongly complimented on their work by the O/BGC. Expenditure 51. Retaliation.	
	7th	5.15m	"Lt." HALL - "T/6" - 2nd enemy T.M. for E.T.M. which was silenced - Very quiet & enemy working party dispersed - M.G. silenced. Retaliation for T.M. which was silenced.	

WAR DIARY
or
INTELLIGENCE SUMMARY.

Army Form C. 2118.

JANUARY — '18.

Place	Date	Hour	Summary of Events and Information	Remarks and references to Appendices
	8th		Expenditure 126.	
		5.15pm	Sniper interfered with wiring party – 10 rounds were fired from ITV III. Cavalry reported Sniper blown up. Did not fire again –	
	9th	1.15am to 1.30am	Retaliation for 7 a.m. M.W. 8 rounds –	
		7.30pm	Section relief	
			Previous night very quiet – no enemy activity	
		2.30am	Expenditure 5 – at M.G. gun silenced	
	10R	4.30pm	Lt. BLACKALL relieved Lt. HALL –	
		2.30pm	Enemy working party dispersed by No 4 Gun.	
		2.30pm	5 Gun retaliated on Camouflage Screen night of C.T.	
		3:30pm	Enemy H.T.M. active on TURNIP LANE No 2 Gun retaliated	
		9.50pm to 10.15pm	Enemy H.T.M. again active on TURNIP LANE and FARM. B.P.T. Nos 1, 2 & 3 retaliated	
			Total Expenditure of the 10th 83 rounds.	
	11-	3.15am	Enemy working party dispersed by No 4 Gun	
		3.30pm	Enemy seen working on new C.T. No 5 Gun fired on them and work ceased.	
		7.15pm	Enemy M.G. silenced by No 6 Gun.	
		7.30 to 11.30pm	Harassing fire was carried out by all guns on enemy front line, new C.T. and support line.	

WAR DIARY
or
INTELLIGENCE SUMMARY.
(Erase heading not required.)

Army Form C. 2118.

JANUARY – 1918.

Instructions regarding War Diaries and Intelligence Summaries are contained in F.S. Regs., Part II. and the Staff Manual respectively. Title pages will be prepared in manuscript.

Place	Date	Hour	Summary of Events and Information	Remarks and references to Appendices
	11th		Attitude of enemy quiet. Practically no retaliation to our fire. Total expenditure 81 rounds.	
	12th	5 a.m.	M.G. silenced by No 6 Gun.	
		6.15 p.m. 7.30 p.m. 8 p.m.	No 2 retaliated to hostile T.M. No 6 silenced M.G. No 4 fired on dugouts at G.S.c. 80.80.	
		9.30 p.m. 12 p.m. 11.30 p.m.	No 4 Gun engaged active enemy T.M. and eventually succeeded in silencing it. During the remainder of the night all guns were active on enemy front line C.T's and support line. Except for a little T.M. and M.G. fire the attitude of the enemy is quiet. Total Expenditure 115 rounds.	
	13th	4 a.m.	Enemy working party dispersed by No 6 Gun.	
		11.30 a.m. 2.30 p.m. 11.30 a.m.	No 6 B was registered on front and support lines. No 6 A was registered on front and support lines. Nos 4 & 6 Guns retaliated to hostile T.M. Owing to activity of our patrols the guns were not able to fire for the greater part of the night. Total Expenditure 49 rounds.	

WAR DIARY or INTELLIGENCE SUMMARY

Army Form C. 2118.

JANUARY - 1918.

Place	Date	Hour	Summary of Events and Information	Remarks and references to Appendices
	13th	6 p.m.	Inter Section Relief.	
	14th	1.30 a.m.	Enemy working party dispersed by No 5 Gun.	
		2 p.m. to 4 a.m.	Nos 1 & 6 Guns retaliated to hostile T.M. fire.	
	15th	2.30 p.m.	2nd Lt. Williams relieved Lt. Blackall	
		—	81 rounds fired in retaliation for T.M. fire —	
	16	—	61 rounds fired. 26 of these on a working party which was dispersed. The remainder in retaliation —	
	17	2.30 a.m.	Minor enterprise carried out by 6th D.G's. No fire was called for. Expenditure 32 – 6.6 Shell on E.M.G.	O.O.9 no 50 attached.
	18th	7 p.m.	Battery relieved by Cav. LTM Batt. On relief Batt. moved to HANCOURT. Accommodated in three NISSON HUTS in very bad condition.	O.O.9 no 51 attached.
	19th	—	Lt. L'ESTRANGE & BLACKALL went to TEMPLEUX to arrange relief with 19th LTMBM.	
	20th	—		
	21st	10.30 a.m.	Battery relieved 17th LTM Batt. marching via ROISEL with half for lunch.	
		7 p.m.	Relief complete, taking over only 8 guns —	
	22nd		Engaged new enemy post. Very successful shooting. Expenditure 12 rounds.	

WAR DIARY
or
INTELLIGENCE SUMMARY.
(Erase heading not required.)

Army Form C. 2118.

Place	Date	Hour	Summary of Events and Information	Remarks and references to Appendices
	23rd		31 rounds fired on new post.	
	24th		NIL. 52 rounds retaliation of hostile T.M. Another gun fired into action at H.Q. dugout	
			FERRET LEFT. Captain HOLME. & LT L'ESTRANGE reconnoitred intended	
			sites for defensive emplacements.	
	25th	3pm	LT. BLACKALL relieved LT HALL. Intersection relief.	
			35 rounds.	
	26th	—	50 rounds - Trench against new work - and M.G.	
		5am	Pte. SMITHERMAN killed by L.T.M. direct hit on centre MAKAROFF emplacement.	
			Breech in gun undamaged & very little damage to emplacement.	
	27	{11pm {3am	H.Q. Bricks TEMPLEUX shelled at intervals with H.2" H.E. Three direct hits in courtyard a surrounding huts. Pte WHITAKER (Runner) wounded in abdomen while on sentry duty. There was no damage. 60 rounds expended.	
			Captain MOLL reconnoitred emplacements forward of an intermediate line.	
	28th	—	80 rounds expended. Captain MOLL & WYNDHAM 72 L'THING & Captain GORD forward emplacement a intermediate line. LT! L'ESTRANGE & WHITE proc	
			emplacements in outpost line.	

Army Form C. 2118.

WAR DIARY
or
INTELLIGENCE SUMMARY. January

(Erase heading not required.)

Instructions regarding War Diaries and Intelligence Summaries are contained in F. S. Regs., Part II and the Staff Manual respectively. Title pages will be prepared in manuscript.

Place	Date	Hour	Summary of Events and Information	Remarks and references to Appendices
	24/1		20 recruits reported in	
	30/1	2.30p	30 recruits. Battery relieved by 72nd L.T.M.Bdy.	O.O.
			Battery on relief moved to HERMIES	
	31/1	—	Inspections & baths — Issue of new clothing	

R Sharp(?)
for O.C. 23 L.T.M.B.

Operation Orders. 51
14/15/1/18

(1) The 73rd L.T.M.B.y will be relieved by the Cav. L.T.M.B.y on the night 17/18

(2) On relief the 73rd L.T.M.B.y will move to Hancourt

(3) Gun Teams will be relieved about 7.P.M. On relief these teams will report to Hancourt Stores

(4) Battery H.Q. less six men will move at 2.P.M.

(5) Guides will be at Crucifix Barnes to meet parties

(6) All stores, maps etc will be handed over, and proper receipts taken. Guns complete less Tool Bags will be handed over.

1. 2/Lt Williams
2. Cav. L.T.M.B.y.
3. File
4. War Diary

C.C. 73 L.T.M.B.y
12/1/18

Tumpleux
Sergt Scott
pte Butcher
" Smitherman
" Watkinson
Lcpl Beale
pte Hope
" Hilton
" Vickers J
" Boulter
" Meader
Cpl Ward
Lcpl Bulley
pte Richards
" Taylor
Lcpl Wooller
pte Wedgfield
" Kenison
" White
" Reynolds
" Clarkin
" Jefferys

Cooks { pte Yates Vickers G
       { " Poole
       { " Flanagan
       { " Mustchin

Billets in Tumpleux Rd

Servants
Farnes
Reid
Powell
Piggott
Jeffers

Secret   Copy No 3

OPERATION ORDERS 50

Ref. Hargicourt 10,000

(1) The Cavalry are going to carry out a minor enterprise on night 16/17-1-18

(2) Objective   M.G. + crew at G8a 10.30

(3) Points of entry   at G8a 10.30 and G8a 30.67

(4) The raid is to be silent and no barrage will be fired unless called for by S.O.S. signal of Gold and Silver Very lights.

(5) Action on S.O.S   The Artillery, Stokes, and M.G. will open a barrage on prearranged targets for five minutes – if this is not sufficient a second light will be put up and the barrage repeated for five minutes.

(6) Targets   No 3 Gun Trench Jn at G8c 15.40.
   A. No 4 Gun } C.T. at G8c 50.90.
   B. No 4 Gun }
      No 5 Gun F.L. at G7B 98.45
   A. No 6 Gun } C.T. at G8a 20.60
   B. No 6 Gun } Jn at G7B 92.62

(7) Rate of fire – 15 rounds per minute.

II

(8) The above targets will be registered today 16th

(9) Zero hour will be notified later

No 1. 2nd D Ow
No 2. 2/Lt Williams
No 3) WAR DIARY
No 4)

[signature]

O.C. 73rd L.T.M. Battery

16-1-18

WAR DIARY
INTELLIGENCE SUMMARY

4th Light Trench Mortar Battery

For the month of February 1918

WAR DIARY
or
INTELLIGENCE SUMMARY.

(Erase heading not required.)

Army Form C. 2118.

February — 1910 —

Place	Date	Hour	Summary of Events and Information	Remarks and references to Appendices
Hervilly to Tinoirbs	Hervilly	—	Battery out in support at HERVILLY. Working parties daily to work on new emplacements etc in RED Line.	
Tinor 15	Templeine	—	Battery relieved 17th L.M.Batt. 2 guns RCOH support — 2 guns in PWD support — H.Q. FERRET Left. Pers H.Q. at TEMPLIEUX & GUERRARD — Lieut SMITH in Forward H.Q.	
Tinor 17		—	1 gun sent to M.A. emplacement FERRET LEFT. Pers H.Q. shelled at 12.A.M. no casualties.	
Tinor 18		—	2g emplacement joined Batt. 21 men returned. Working parties to HARGICOURT. Underseckn relief. Lut BLACKALL returned.	
" 19		—		
22		—	Guns in POMO & FERRET relieved by 172 L.M.Batt. Rearranged of 13th Ledgr — LIEUT HOLT A/Plk. Batt Hohim to lucuit.	

WAR DIARY
or
INTELLIGENCE SUMMARY.

Army Form C. 2118.

Place	Date	Hour	Summary of Events and Information	Remarks and references to Appendices
	23.	—	One gun withdrawn from COCOA. to INDIAN POST. One gun sent to ANTRENERES POST — Lt SMITH relieved Forward Hill moved to INDIAN Post. Intersection relief.	
	24.		One gun to VALLEY Post — One gun to HARDY Bank and one more gun to ARTERNERES — Total 6 guns in position — Intersection	
	25		Cpl PLUCK fired two rounds at an aeroplane Ammunition sent up to new trenches	
	26		More ammunition sent up — 12 midnight R.G.S. sent up also the front — No action followed —	
	27		All guns were registered — Tm PLIEUX heavily shelled at 4.30 p.m. LIEUT. WILLIAMS returned from leave LIEUT L'ESTRANGE sent to HERVILLY to prepare on LIEUT BLACKALL relieved	

Place	Date	Hour	Summary of Events and Information	Remarks and references to Appendices
Iras	28		Cpl HODGKISS fired at an aeroplane nearly hitting it – W H Murphy Lt. 73rd W.M. Batt.	

73rd Brigade.
24th Division.

73rd LIGHT TRENCH MORTAR BATTERY

MARCH 1918

WAR DIARY
INTELLIGENCE SUMMARY

Army Form C. 2118.

Place	Date	Hour	Summary of Events and Information	Remarks and references to Appendices
Continued			2nd Light Trench Mortar Battery for the month of March 1918	

WAR DIARY or INTELLIGENCE SUMMARY.

Army Form C. 2118.

Place	Date	Hour	Summary of Events and Information	Remarks and references to Appendices
Templeux	1/3/18	6 p.m.	Battery relieved by the 107th L.I.M. Battery On the relief Battery proceeded to ROISEL.	
	2/3/18		Battery moved to VRAIGNES occupying "B" Camp Lieut L'Estrange reported from Artillery.	
	2/3-20/3		Battery at half hour's notice at VRAIGNES. On 16th Capt MOLL went on leave Lieut L'ESTRANGE took command of Battery	
	21/3/18	5:30am	Alarm action given by Brigade 6.30 Battery stood down	
		3:30pm	Alarm action again given and again washed out	
	22/3/18		As the 9th Division was fighting on ahead all stores etc. were ordered to be destroyed	
		4 p.m.	Battery ordered to proceed to MERICOURT where Brigade was concentrating	
		7pm	Battery ordered on outpost covering Brigade at PEUILLY outposts were taken up and patrols pushed out towards PEUILLY	
	23/3/18	1:30am	Battery retired to take outpost line ESTREES to VRAIGNES	
		4:30am	Battery retired to rejoin Brigade at FLEZ arriving here 7.0 a.m. Battery ordered to prolong the line Brigade was holding beyond GUIZANCOURT	

A6945 Wt. W11422/M1160 350,000 12/16 D. D. & L. Forms/C./2118/14.

WAR DIARY
or
INTELLIGENCE SUMMARY.

Army Form C. 2118.

(Erase heading not required.)

Place	Date	Hour	Summary of Events and Information	Remarks and references to Appendices
			In position at 8.30am facing EAST	
		9:30am	Brigade was ordered to withdraw to the SOMME taking up a position at FALBY within the Battery dug in on the right of the River	
		1pm	Battery was ordered to cross the SOMME and proceed to MARCHELEPOT on the way Battery came under shell fire and Pte EVANS was wounded. Shortly after passing LICOURT Battery was ordered back to take up position covering crossings of the SOMME	
	24/3/18	5am	Division was relieved by 8th Division and the Battery ordered to CHAULNES	
		3pm	Battery ordered to PUZEAUX in close support to 9th R. Sussex	
	25/3/18	6am	Brigade moved forward to bur DRESLINCOURT-CURCHY to cooperate in counter attack with the French DRESLINCOURT was found to be strongly held by the enemy and the Battery was ordered to make a defensive Front the Sussex ‍taking up work the 1st R.F's opposite BERSAUCOURT Battery took up position along a trench running between these two places coming under heavy machine gun fire	
		11:30am	1st R.F's withdrew and the enemy occupied BERSAUCOURT and were also occupying the	

WAR DIARY or INTELLIGENCE SUMMARY.

Army Form C. 2118.

(Erase heading not required.)

Place	Date	Hour	Summary of Events and Information	Remarks and references to Appendices
			railway station on the DRESLINCOURT - COURCHY road	
		12.00pm	Brigade incorporated to withdraw and take up positions the previous night that was. In doing this heavy casualties Corpl PUCK wounded in the back had to be abandoned to the enemy. During the retirement Battery got scattered and only 20 reassembled at PUZEAUX casualties in this action were 10 wounded. A further withdrawal to HALLU was ordered and the Battery formed rearguard to Brigade. This was afterwards countermanded and it was required to PUZEAUX the Brigade withdrew to trenches on the PUNCHY - CHAULNES road	
		7.30pm	The enemy having occupied PUZEAUX the Brigade withdrew to trenches on the PUNCHY - CHAULNES road	
	26/3/18	3 a.m.	A further withdrawal was ordered to the HALLU - CHAULNES line where we found orders and a new platoon of reinforcements was attached to the Battery	
		6 a.m.	Division withdrew to the ROSIERES - ROUVROY line the Battery taking up a position on the right flank of the Brigade near FOUQUESCOURT. About midday the enemy was seen advancing in strength but later on they withdrew as there was much movement of the enemy who this night W & Coy Sussex was attached to us seen during the night close to our position	

| 27/3/18 | 8.30 a.m. | The enemy having dug in machine gun positions within 200 yds of our line commenced an attack chiefly against the right of the right of the Battery the 61st reinforcement Company was holding the line from the centre of whose position ran a very deep communication trench to some advanced works. This was not held and the enemy effected an entrance into this company's positions half of whom withdrew along our trench the enemy came along the trench as far as the right part of the Battery where a brisk engagement took place lasting till 1.0 p.m. meanwhile the enemy working round our right flank managed to get a machine gun in position in some high mounds enfilading our trench and soon the garrison of this part of the trench were all either killed or wounded including two Lewis Gun teams of A Coy 9th R Sussex. By about 1 pm the Middlesex Regt who went to reserve were in position covering the gap in our line and the OC Battery ordered a withdrawal along the trench to position of the 9th R. Sussex. In this withdrawal 2/Lt Smith, L/Cpl Trojan who was killed, and Pte Sanford distinguished themselves in delaying the enemy and so allowing the garrison to get clear. A block was formed and held by the Battery and other reinforcements picked up until the Northamptonshire position took place then and when a further withdrawal down to the Northamptonshire position took place |

SUMMARY OF EVENTS.

DATE	HOUR	
28/3/18	3 am	The enemy attempted no further advance that day. The Battery had suffered heavy casualties. 4 killed and 5 wounded. Brigade was ordered to retire to the CAIX - LE QUESNEL line but the enemy occupied LE QUESNAL at 5 pm a further retirement was ordered via BEAUCOURT MEZIERES to VILLIERS from here after dark a further withdrawal was made to CASTEL. The Battery bivouacking that night in the Bois de SENCET
29/3/18		In the afternoon the Brigade took up a position covering the enemy at CASTEL and from there marched after dark via HAILLES to THEZY Enroute they billetted Battery remained in billets
30/3/18		
31/3/18		At dusk the Battery took up position on high ground N.W of THEENNES supporting the bridge head companys at that place

WAR DIARY
INTELLIGENCE SUMMARY

Army Form C. 2118.

Place	Date	Hour	Summary of Events and Information	Remarks and references to Appendices

continued

4th Bde Light Trench Mortar Battery
for the month of
April 1918

WAR DIARY
or
INTELLIGENCE SUMMARY.
(Erase heading not required.)

Army Form C. 2118.

Place	Date	Hour	Summary of Events and Information	Remarks and references to Appendices
	1-4-18 to 4-4-18		Battery still attached to 9th Royal Sussex held high ground N of THENNES and BERTHEAUCOURT	
	5-4-18		Moved to BOIS DE GENTELLES and held ground S of it	
	6-4-18	9pm	Marched to LONGEAU	
	7-4-18	5am	Bused to SALEUX	
		7pm	Entrained to ST VALERY	
	8-4-18		Marched to FRIVILLE. Capt MOLL rejoined Battery	
	10-4-18		Marched to ST MARC Capt Moll handed over Battery to LIEUT L'ESTRANGE	
	11-4-18		Battery made up to 96 strong. Lt SHEMMONDS - 13Fr MIDDLESEX & 2/Lt DAVIS - 9re ROYAL SUSSEX attached	
			Entrained to BEUGIN	
	14-4-18 17-4-18 to 25-4-18		Training at BEUGIN when Lt BLACKALL returned from leave	
	29-4-18		Marched up to the line to relieve. Orders cancelled & returned to BEUGIN	
	30-4-18		Marched to LES BREBIS	

WAR DIARY
INTELLIGENCE SUMMARY
(Erase heading not required.)

Army Form C. 2118.

Place	Date	Hour	Summary of Events and Information	Remarks and references to Appendices
Fourth Army			4th Australian Light Trench Mortar Battery From the month of May 1918	

Army Form C. 2118.

WAR DIARY 73rd M.M. Batt.
or
INTELLIGENCE SUMMARY. April

(Erase heading not required.)

Place	Date	Hour	Summary of Events and Information	Remarks and references to Appendices
Hill 70 – (LOOS)	1st	2.30 pm	Six teams and twenty four men, relieved the 8th Bn. L.M. Both in the line in the Hill 70 sector. Dispositions. Guns forward by day withdrawn to defensive positions at stand to in the morning. Two officers in the line. H.Q. at Railway Trench. Details at Les Brebis.	
	2 – 8.		Ordinary trench routine.	
	9.		Received news of intending enemy attack. Guns got ready to reserve emplacements – extra ammunition got up. No attack developed.	
	10.		Ordinary trench routine continued.	
	11.			
	12.		17th M Bath relieved our two right guns – Dispositions were three guns on the left in forward emplacements. One gun in reserve – on the right two gun sited for counter attack work.	
	15.	9.30-	No 3 gun had a premature bursting 2 killed 8 wounded. Cause unknown.	
	20.		Lt. Smith rejoined from hospital & came up the line. H.Q. forward – no casualties.	

Abbrey Capt.
73 LM Batt.

War Diary
for month of June.

13m Light Trench Mortar Battery

73 Light T.M.B.

WAR DIARY or INTELLIGENCE SUMMARY

Army Form C. 2118.

June 1918.

Place	Date	Hour	Summary of Events and Information	Remarks and references to Appendices
Line	2nd		Normal Section Relief.	
"	6th		Normal Section Relief.	
Les Brebis	10th		Details moved from Les Brebis to Bully-Grenay, including Officers' Mess.	
			At Blackall and Batty S.M. Scott proceeded to recce on the ground.	
			Special arrangements with regard to ammunition in case of enemy attack which was notified as likely within 48 hours.	
			Normal relief carried out in the lines.	
	14		Normal relief.	
	16th		Lt Blackall and Batty S.M. Scott returned from leave.	
	17th		Two guns registered from Apthe Alley on enemy position at MINT SAP, and	
			Three guns in BOIS HUGO for a raid.	
	19th		Ammunition specially prepared for raid at emplacements in HORSE MEET hit	
			direct by S.G. Dug-out blown up and S.O.R. burned. Two guns blown up.	
			No casualties amongst site.	
			Shot carried out as registered barrage raid by N.M.Lancs Rgt at 6 p.m. Three hundred and sixty rounds expended, and no casualties. By that infantry were obtained.	

Army Form C. 2118.

WAR DIARY
or
INTELLIGENCE SUMMARY.
(Erase heading not required.)

Instructions regarding War Diaries and Intelligence Summaries are contained in F. S. Regs., Part II. and the Staff Manual respectively. Title pages will be prepared in manuscript.

Place	Date	Hour	Summary of Events and Information	Remarks and references to Appendices
Line	20th		First three cases of "Trench Fever" admitted to hospital from this unit.	
	21st		Capt L'Estrange admitted to hospital. Lt. Blackall took over command.	
	22nd		Normal Relief. Series of reserve emplacements sited for defence by localities.	
	24th		Normal Relief. Lt. Blackall admitted to hospital with prevailing P.U.O.	
			Lt. Smith took over command.	
	27th		Line H.Q. withdrawn from Railway Alley to PREVITE CASTLE (Advanced)	
			H.Q. withdrawn from RAILWAY ALLEY FORWARD to TOSH ALLEY. Coy H.Q.	
			teams withdrawn from line to reserve positions in TOSH ALLEY, LOOS	
			TRENCH and SCOTS ALLEY. Strafing carried out nightly from these	
			two forward bay travelling guns. New return and ammunition limps	
			maintained at BREWERY, LOOS.	
	30th		Normal Relief.	

Sgd M.Flint
Lt
7/M.B.
73

WAR DIARY

INTELLIGENCE SUMMARY.

(Erase heading not required.)

Army Form C. 2118.

Place	Date	Hour	Summary of Events and Information	Remarks and references to Appendices
Continued			4our Light Trench Mortar Battery for the month of July 1918	

WAR DIARY
or
INTELLIGENCE SUMMARY.
(Erase heading not required.)

Army Form C. 2118.

July 73rd LMBatt

Place	Date	Hour	Summary of Events and Information	Remarks and references to Appendices
Hill 70 area	July		The Battery was in the line the whole month. Ordinary trench warfare carrying out reliefs every four days commencing on the 11th	
	11th	—	Capt Flahery returned from hospital & took over command	
	15		2nd Blackall returned from hospital	
	16th		One gun taken from Cameron and put in the HYTHE TUNNEL	
	22nd		Two guns supported raid by 7th Scottish 190 rounds	
	23rd		While leading a limber at B keep in LOOS with select ammunition Sergt GRIWOOD Ptes BINFIELD & BARKER were killed by the second blowing up. Mules killed and driver wounded —	

Whitham/s Capt
73rd LMBatt.

WAR DIARY
INTELLIGENCE SUMMARY
(Erase heading not required.)

Army Form C. 2118.

10th Australian Light Trench Mortar Battery

For the month of August 1918

Army Form C. 2118.

WAR DIARY
or
INTELLIGENCE SUMMARY.
(Erase heading not required.)

Instructions regarding War Diaries and Intelligence Summaries are contained in F. S. Regs., Part II. and the Staff Manual respectively. Title pages will be prepared in manuscript.

Place	Date	Hour	Summary of Events and Information	Remarks and references to Appendices
HW 701	1/8/18		Team relieving in the line	
	2/8/18		2nd Lieut. BERRY & 2/Lieut DAVIS returned to station this	
	3/8/18		19 O.R's joined reinforcement	
			A two section was sent out	
	5/8/18		Team relieving in the line	
	7/8/18		Capt. L'ESTRANGE, M.C. proceeded on leave to U.K.	
	8/8/18	2/30p	Two guns in HORSE ABBEY fired 706 rounds in support of attack by 5th DORSETS (11th DIVISION).	
	9/8/18		Team relieving in the line	
	13/8/18		Team relieved in the line	
	17/8/18		Team relieved in the line	
	21/8/18		Team relieved in the line	
	23/8/18		Capt. L'ESTRANGE, M.C. returned from leave	
	25/8/18		Team relieved in the line	
	27/8/18	11am	46th & Lt. W. Boxley Sergt. SMITH & L/Cpl. GREEN wounded, remained this unit	

WAR DIARY
or
INTELLIGENCE SUMMARY.
(Erase heading not required.)

Army Form C. 2118.

Place	Date	Hour	Summary of Events and Information	Remarks and references to Appendices
LIEVIN	27/8/18		This Battery relieved 6th L.T.M. Battery in its Sector 2 guns forward in "Ouvrage" Zone 3 guns ground in Black Row	
	28/8/18		Lieut. S. SMITH and 1 O.R. proceeded on leave to U.K.	
	31/8/18		Teams figures to the Rim. 2 moved guns go into Black Row.	

H. Danny, Captain
Comdg. 7th Lighte Trench Mortar Battery

13th Light T. M. Battery

War Diary

Army Form C. 2118.

WAR DIARY
or
INTELLIGENCE SUMMARY.
(Erase heading not required.)

Instructions regarding War Diaries and Intelligence Summaries are contained in F. S. Regs, Part II. and the Staff Manual respectively. Title pages will be prepared in manuscript.

Place	Date	Hour	Summary of Events and Information	Remarks and references to Appendices
LENS	1.9.18		LIEUT. SHEMMONDS proceeded to GASCOURSE.	
	"		Information received that enemy was evacuating LENS. Orders received to push forward patrols.	
	2.9.18		GREEN CRASSIER occupied by us and advanced posts established in LENS. 2 no 3" STOKES GUNS totalled in our old front line.	
	6.9.18		Fairly settled with YELLOW CROSS GAS, no casualties.	
	7.9.18		One signaller joined from Battalion Re Brigade.	
	8.9.18		Capt L'ESTRANGE M.C. & twenty-five new proceeded to KMMQUEFFLES FARM to train in conjunction with infantry.	
	9		LIEUT. CHEMMONDS returned from course.	
	10.9.18		Teams relieved and others in line.	
	B.9.18 6.30 a.m.		Direct hit received on mule horse from while turning on LENS STATION. Casualties – Three O.Rs killed, two O.Rs wounded. Gun totally destroyed.	
	14.9.18		Section relieved others in line. No 1 section to NOULETTE WOOD for training.	
	15.9.18		Gun positions taken over from 42nd T.M.By.	

Army Form C. 2118.

WAR DIARY
or
INTELLIGENCE SUMMARY.
(Erase heading not required.)

Instructions regarding War Diaries and Intelligence Summaries are contained in F. S. Regs., Part II. and the Staff Manual respectively. Title pages will be prepared in manuscript.

Place	Date	Hour	Summary of Events and Information	Remarks and references to Appendices
LENS	18.9.18		Teams relive each other in line.	
	19.9.18		Between 2.0 & 3.00. 5.9c & 4.2s Bty H.Q at LIEVEN. Direct hit on Bty H.Q. No Cas x Ves.	
	22.9.18		No 1 section relieve No 2 section in line. No 2 section proceeded NOULETTE WOOD for training. Heavy rain during afternoon & evening.	
	26.9.18		Hun attack along Divisional Front.	
	30.9.18		Battery relieved by 175th L.T.M.B, proceeded to ROMERSIN Billets Rest. night 30.9.18 - 1.10.18.	
	1.10.18		Entrained at MERCIN proceeded to MONCHCURT, hence by M.T. BOUT de PRES where the battery was billeted.	

[signature]
Captain,
Commdg 173rd L.T.M. Battery

73rd LIGHT MORTAR BATTERY ORDER No 107

Ref maps
SHEET 44 & B.
1/40000

Copy No 3

1. The 24th Division is being relieved in the line by the 58th Division.

2. The 73rd L.M. Bty. will be relieved by the 175th L.M.B. on the afternoon of the 30th Sept.
   On relief the fwd L.Mb. 15tg (less transport for which separate orders will be issued) will proceed to HERSIN, prior to the Divn. being transferred to another area on Oct 1st.

3. Entraining point for trops. & the section will be the .... - ...... -SOUCHEZ Road, head of column at ... fit. Sept 30.

4. Men & items under Lieut Smith will march to HERSIN leaving at 9.15am. Route - During the Mx HOULETTE - BOYEFFLES to HERSIN. Dress Marching Order.

5. LIGHT SHEPHERDS will leave HERSIN by train at 8am and report to Staff Captain, Area Commandants office LOZINCK. Sgt GOODWIN Nco. and RUNNER will go forward to HERSIN on morning Sept 30, and take over billets from 73rd L.M.Bty. He will be return to meet and guide the section.

6. Blankets will be rolled ready for loading up by 9.a.m.

7. A guide will be placed on the HERSIN - .... Road from ..... onwards to meet buses.

8. All maps (except 44913 /40000) Defence schemes, photographs, trench stores, ammunition etc will be handed over & receipt obtained.

In addition the two guns in forward positions will be handed over viz:—
- Toolbags complete
- Min number
- Cartridge baskettes
- Gun slings

9. Relieved detachment will report relief complete to forward HQ.

Issued 9 a.m.

Capt
Commanding
93rd L.M.B. Bty.

Copy No 1 File
2. 93rd L.B.
3. War Diary
4. 7cl HQ
5. No 1 Section
6. Batt. Q.M.S.

WAR DIARY

INTELLIGENCE SUMMARY.
(Erase heading not required.)

Army Form C. 2118

Place	Date	Hour	Summary of Events and Information	Remarks and references to Appendices
Contescourt			Nil Bronchyte Trench Mortar Battery for the month of October 1918	

WAR DIARY or INTELLIGENCE SUMMARY

Army Form C. 2118

Place	Date	Hour	Summary of Events and Information	Remarks and references to Appendices
Bout du Pres	October 1st to 6th		In Billets	
	6th	6 pm	Entrained at MONDICOURT	
	7th	1.30 am	Detrained at FREMICOURT marched to Camp near MOEUVRES	
		5 pm	Marched to CANTAING	
	8th	5 pm	Marched to MONT-sur-L'OEUVRE	
	9th	5 am	Marched to NIERGNIES — in support to 72nd I.B. One section attached to Royal Sussex Regt and One section to 7th I.B. hand Grenade stock one company of Enemy at AWOINGT. Railway bridge at AWOINGT was subjected to heavy shelling. It was much such the village where H.Q. formed offices front of the village where H.Q. formed offices	
	10th	9.30	marched to Q marching to CAUDRIE to CAUDRY where H.Q. formed	
		6 am	The Bunnes was reported One Battn rejoined its Unit moved to TOUR au LIEU where the remaining section rejoined Battn	

Army Form C. 2118.

WAR DIARY
or
INTELLIGENCE SUMMARY.
(Erase heading not required.)

Instructions regarding War Diaries and Intelligence Summaries are contained in F. S. Regs., Part II. and the Staff Manual respectively. Title pages will be prepared in manuscript.

Place	Date	Hour	Summary of Events and Information	Remarks and references to Appendices
RIEUX	11th		Bn 17th I.B. Convoy stopped & Bty. went into Bieus nr RIEUX	
	12th		In Billets in RIEUX	
	13th			
AVESNES	14th	10am	Marches to Bieus in AVESNES	
	16th		Advance party proceed to CAUROIR to Bieus. O.C. Unit with two returning 4 A.M. August in supporting 72nd I.B. where Bty. marches	
	17th		Section returned to AVESNES	
			to CAUROIR.	
	18th		Section was armed with 2 Rifle "Minenwerfer" replacing two 57th guns.	
	26th		Bty. marched to HAUSSY & thorough audit its own of its ammunition	

W. Khant Captain
3rd F.T.M. Battery
Commdg.

WAR DIARY

INTELLIGENCE SUMMARY

Confidential

9th Light Trench Mortar Battery
for the month of
November 1916

WAR DIARY
or
INTELLIGENCE SUMMARY.
(Erase heading not required.)

Army Form C. 2118.

73rd LIGHT TRENCH MORTAR BATTERY.

Place	Date	Hour	Summary of Events and Information	Remarks and references to Appendices
HAUSSEY	1/11/18	—	REST BILLETS	
— do —	2/11/18	2p	March to BERTRERAIN & GIELLER. Lieut. N. BLACHAR Proceeded on Leave to U.K.	
BERTRERAIN	3/11/18	3pm	March to MARESCHES & GIELLER	
MARESCHES	4/11/18	3.30	Move through VILLERS-POL to Sunken Road - North of Capt. ETIENY moved forward Two Stokes Gun Teams under Capt. ETIENY moved forward to support the Infantry.	
		6am	One MINENWERFER & Capt. H.H.L'ESTRANGE M.C. followed up a a the MINENWERFER & VILLERS POL Road & GENLAIN - VILLERS POL Road observing that the 9th ROYAL SUSSEX REGT were held up by hostile M.P. fire further forward to engage, picking up two MINENWERFERS on the way - Gun Came into action at 300 yds. range engaged the M.G. It was falsely reported that the enemy were making a Counter-attack & both guns opened rapid On Enemy trenches - reports accurate meanwhile the two Stokes team had collected

WAR DIARY
or
INTELLIGENCE SUMMARY.
(Erase heading not required.)

Army Form C. 2118.

73rd LIGHT TRENCH MORTAR BATTERY.

Place	Date	Hour	Summary of Events and Information	Remarks and references to Appendices
WARGNIES-L-PETIT	5-11-18	7am	Tear down to Cage 46 prisoners - also 2 Heavy M.G. Post where came into action on the right of the MINENWERFER Pm. The enemy retired over the run through WARGNIES-L-GRAND & gun were not called on again until the evening. Hair Lieut. P. Smith brought up H.Q. to the gun. Casualties 2 O.R's wounded.	
		7/-	The 2 MINENWERFER Gun went forward through WARGNIES-L-GRAND & took up position for the night coming into BAVAI Road	
			Battery were relieved by 17th Inf. Bde. Battery moved to WARGNIES-L-PETIT	
— do —	6-11-18		Billet in WARGNIES-L-PETIT	
BAVAI	7-11-18	3p	Move to BAVAI - Billets.	
LE LOUVOIN	8-11-18	2p	Move to LE LOUVOIN - Billets.	
LE BASVENTS	9-11-18	5am	Move to LE BASVENTS Coming up in Line on left of 72nd L.B.	

WAR DIARY
or
INTELLIGENCE SUMMARY
(Erase heading not required.)

Army Form C. 2118.

73rd LIGHT TRENCH MORTAR BATTERY.

No. ....
Date. ....

Place	Date	Hour	Summary of Events and Information	Remarks and references to Appendices
FLORICAMP			Hostly proved the enemy to the MAUBURGE — MONS road reaching there 12 noon. Operation finished for the day — Gilleur in FLORICAMP	
FIENGIES	10.11.18	10am	Relieved by 20th Division & Battery marched to FIENGIES	
BAVAI-LOUVIGNIES	11.11.18	10am	Marched to BAVAI-LOUVIGNIES. During the march news was received that the Armistice was signed.	
			Lieut. R.W. HERR proceeded on leave to U.K.	
	12.11.18		BAVAI-LOUVIGNIES	
	13.11.18			
	14.11.18			
	15.11.18			
	16.11.18			
WARGNIES-le-GRAND	17.11.18	10:30am	Move to WARGNIES-le-GRAND.	
PROVEY	18.11.18	9am	Move to PROVEY	
ANICHE	19.11.18	10:30am	Move to ANICHE & Billets.	
	20.11.18		ANICHE.	
	21.11.18			
	22.11.18			
	23.11.18			
	24.11.18			
RUMEGIES	25.11.18	9am	Move to RUMEGIES	
MOUCHIN	26.11.18	10:30am	Moved to MOUCHIN	
	27.11.18		— do —	
	28.11.18		— do —	
	29.11.18		— do —	
	30.11.18		All personnel attached to Battery returned to their battalion.	

Commdg. 73rd L.T.M. Battery. Captain

WAR DIARY
or
INTELLIGENCE SUMMARY.
(Erase heading not required.)

Army Form C. 2118.

War Diary
13 L.T.M. Battery

January

WAR DIARY
or
INTELLIGENCE SUMMARY.
(Erase heading not required.)

Army Form C. 2118.

Place	Date	Hour	Summary of Events and Information	Remarks and references to Appendices
MOUCHIN	Dec 1		C/Sgt "Hugo" Scott & L/Sgt C Goodwin & L/Sgt C Smith transferred to Home Establishment	
	4		Lecture to all Educational instructors in the Brigade RFA in Schoolroom.	
	5		Memorial Service for the late John Price RA Battery was formed. Service conducted by Rev. A. Benton in the Schoolroom	
	9		Educational Classes commenced	
	12		Orders issued for two gunners to proceed to demobilization centre.	
	13		Pte. Millen and Gnr. Sheldon left for demobilization centre.	
	18		Battery moved to billets in TAINTIGNES.	
TAINTIGNES	29		Capt. H.H. L'Strange moved to RUMES with Brigade Orchestra	

[signature] Lut
[signature] O.C. 75/15 MA

WAR DIARY
INTELLIGENCE SUMMARY
(Erase heading not required.)

Army Form C. 2118.

161st Howitzer
13th Australian Light Trench Mortar Battery
For the month of
January 1919

Army Form C. 2118.

WAR DIARY
or
INTELLIGENCE SUMMARY.
(Erase heading not required.)

Instructions regarding War Diaries and Intelligence Summaries are contained in F. S. Regs., Part II. and the Staff Manual respectively. Title pages will be prepared in manuscript.

Place	Date	Hour	Summary of Events and Information	Remarks and references to Appendices
TANTIGNES	2/4/19		2/Lieut. R.W. Kerr admitted to Hospital	
	20/4/19		No. 22844 Pte. J. Small proceeded for demobilization to I Corps Concentration Camp	
	22/4/19		No. 23143. Cpl. Camp H. and 23426 Pte. Noel W. proceeded to I Corps Concentration Camp for demobilization	

C.B. Blackett
Lieut. for Capt.
Commdg. "B" 73rd Light Mortar Bty.

www.ingramcontent.com/pod-product-compliance
Lightning Source LLC
Chambersburg PA
CBHW081453160426
43193CB00013B/2464